BUSINESS DESIGN TOOLS FOR STRATEGY AND INNOVATION

ENTREPRENEURSHIP BY DESIGN

D1671223

Written by: Mario A. Varon and Fernando G. Alberti

strategique

Entrepreneurship by Design
ISBN: 9781797710273

strategique
www.strategique.us
info@strategique.us

BUSINESS DESIGN TOOLS FOR STRATEGY AND INNOVATION

ENTREPRENEURSHIP BY DESIGN *WORKBOOK*

Entrepreneurship
BY DESIGN

Entrepreneurship by design is not only a rich set of tools to design your future business, it is also a framework that will help you make analyses, brainstorming and fine-tuning on it. The book applies a business design approach to facilitate who are planning either to launch their next startup or a new business inside a corporate setting.

Entrepreneurship by design offers a practical hands-on experience, with over 40 different tools that can be used individually or as a step-by-step process to help entrepreneurs and intrapreneurs achieve their goals.

CONTENTS

ENTREPRENEURIAL MINDSET

CUSTOMER DEVELOPMENT

INDUSTRY RESEARCH

VALUE PROPOSITION

MARKET VALIDATION

BUSINESS MODEL

CONTENTS

BRAND IDENTITY

FINANCIAL MODEL

BUSINESS STORYTELLING

Your Journey Starts
HERE

YOU CANNOT DO
SOMETHING JUST
FOR THE MONEY. YOU
HAVE TO DO THINGS
YOU BELIEVE IN AND
EVENTUALLY YOU WILL
MAKE MONEY.

— MIUCCIA PRADA

My Breakthrough Idea

On our daily basis we face multiple problems and challenges, and we think about how we can improve a situation, or how can we do something easier, faster or cheaper. We hope, we dream, and we use our imagination to create new things.

From putting together the outfit will wear in the morning, to the way we get our things done, we are always developing ideas. Some ideas are like shooting stars, others stick in our minds, and we think and talk about them all the time. Those are the ideas we really care about, the ones we firmly believe will break through the status quo and become the next big thing.

Sketching and writing down your ideas will help you visualize, improve and developing them even further.

Start by synthesizing the main concept behind your idea. Make sure it is clear enough so other people can understand them.

Then, define who will be the main users and clients of your idea and what problem are you helping them solve; how this idea could be financially sustainable and its business model; and what resources do you have that will help you develop it.

Finally, create a visual sketch of your idea, showing everything you want your idea to be, how it will look, how it works, and how it can be used, etc.

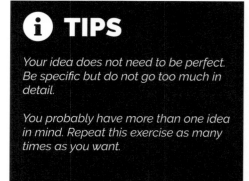

ⓘ TIPS

Your idea does not need to be perfect. Be specific but do not go too much in detail.

You probably have more than one idea in mind. Repeat this exercise as many times as you want.

CONCEPT

USERS

BUSINESS MODEL

RESOURCES

VISUALIZE

LIFE MAP

Our life experiences shaped who we are today, and why do we do the things we do. Throughout our lives we collect a series of memorable moments, both positive and challenging, that help us become the person we are.

These experiences and events come from different aspects of our lives, including our childhood, our school and career choices, and our life outside work. Some of those experiences have a strong significance and impact on us that have a special place in our lives and we keep going back to them for inspiration, motivation or strength.

Gather stories from your past experiences to identify the moments that have shaped your life and made you the person you are today.

Write a specific memorable, positive or challenging story from your life, following a chronological order and write down the year it happened.

Make sure to have stories from your early years, your professional and social life. You should have at least 3 to 6 stories from each category to create your own comprehensive life map.

Capture the emotions you felt and what you learn from each one of them and why this experience is important for your life.

 **TIPS**

Try not to focus too much on the negative aspects of your life and its implications, instead focus on the learnings you have gathered from these experiences.

Identify any emerging patterns on your way of thinking, feeling and behaving.

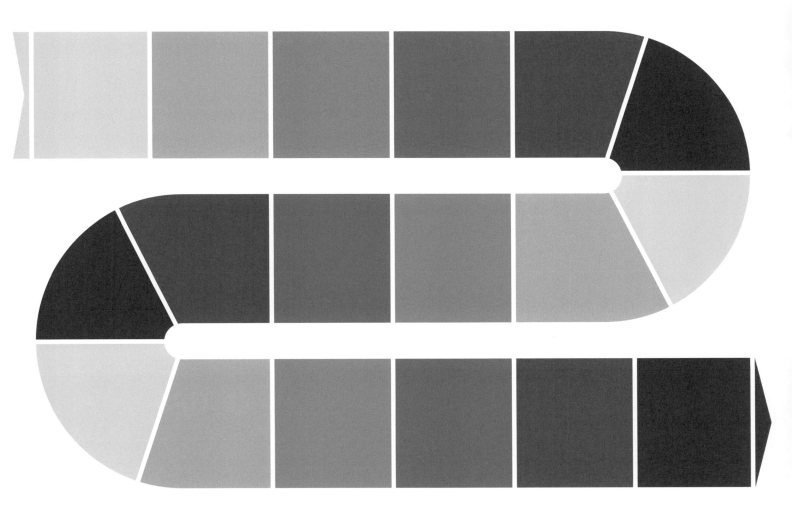

SKILLS MAP

Before starting any new project, it is very important to assess what skills you (and your team) have to offer. Knowing your strengths and limitations will help you identify the external resources you will need to successfully launch your idea.

Some people are better at doing some things than others, as we develop our skills based on our experiences and in everything we do (work, education, hobbies, volunteer work, etc). The goal is to find a good balance between your entrepreneurial traits, and your personal and professional skills with the ones of your team members.

Reflect about your work experience, expertise and skills, strengths, weaknesses and entrepreneurial traits. It is important to be honest, a lack of a particular skill will eventually be noticed and might delay your progress.

Rate your level of each one of the skills presented in the worksheet from 0 (low) to 5 (high).

Connect the dots between each skill to create a radar type graph.

Using a different color, repeat the exercise for each member of your team.

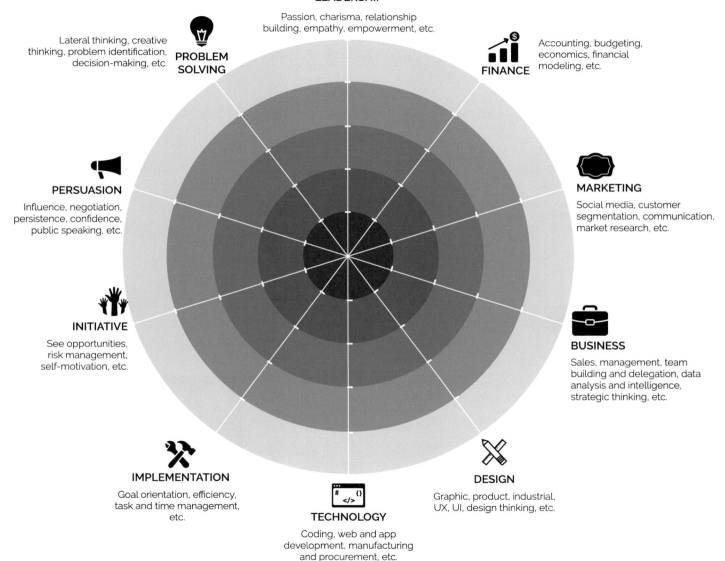

LEADERSHIP
Passion, charisma, relationship building, empathy, empowerment, etc.

PROBLEM SOLVING
Lateral thinking, creative thinking, problem identification, decision-making, etc.

FINANCE
Accounting, budgeting, economics, financial modeling, etc.

PERSUASION
Influence, negotiation, persistence, confidence, public speaking, etc.

MARKETING
Social media, customer segmentation, communication, market research, etc.

INITIATIVE
See opportunities, risk management, self-motivation, etc.

BUSINESS
Sales, management, team building and delegation, data analysis and intelligence, strategic thinking, etc.

IMPLEMENTATION
Goal orientation, efficiency, task and time management, etc.

TECHNOLOGY
Coding, web and app development, manufacturing and procurement, etc.

DESIGN
Graphic, product, industrial, UX, UI, design thinking, etc.

PERSONAL MISSION STATEMENT

Before starting a new project or bringing an idea to life, it is good to know your motivation to do so and why are you so passionate about it. During your entrepreneurial journey you will face many ups and down, and it is that sense of purpose will make you thrive and keep pushing towards fulfilling your goals.

A clear personal mission statement will help you to inspire and motivate people to believe in you and support your idea.

Reflect on your life map (individually or with a partner) and identify common themes and patterns among the different moments.

Categorize those patterns in: values, the principles you live by; passion, what you love and enjoy to do; aspirations, what you hope to experience and achieve; and uniqueness, the things that make you stand out.

Analyze them to uncover what is your contribution to the world and what is the impact of that contribution, and how your actions are perceived by others.

Combine your contribution and impact to create your own personal mission statement.

TIPS

Avoid using jargon and technical language. Your personal mission statement is personal and is not a job description.

Test a few times your statement. Say it out loud and share it with people, iterate it until it feels "right".

VALUES

PASSIONS

ASPIRATIONS

UNIQUENESS

CONTRIBUTION

IMPACT

CONNECTION MAP

To keep your idea moving forward you will need to identify any potential stakeholders (investors, supporters, suppliers, mentors, etc.) or connections that will help you and your team to reach your goals.

Mapping your network will help you keep track of people you and your team are connected with and explore opportunities to capitalize based on their interest and expertise; as well as to recognize in which areas you will need to get introductions or connections.

Visualize your personal and professional connections in different fields relevant for your entrepreneurial journey.

Write down the name and contact information of people and organizations that you have access to.

Organize them by categories starting with your first-degree connections, then add acquaintances and any other potential connections.

Use a different color to target the people you will need to be introduced to and who could make that connection happen.

ⓘ TIPS

Combine in one map all your team connections.

Keep this chart on a visible place and updated regularly.

INDUSTRY

ACADEMIA

BUSINESS

FUNDING

INSTITUTIONS

MEDIA

CUSTOMER
DEVELOPMENT

GET CLOSER THAN EVER TO YOUR CUSTOMERS. SO CLOSE THAT YOU TELL THEM WHAT THEY NEED WELL BEFORE THEY REALIZE IT THEMSELVES.

– STEVE JOBS

SOCIAL MEDIA BEHAVIOR

Knowing your potential customers and users is very important when developing a new idea Understanding their behavior, needs and desires will help you design and build products and services that match their expectations and aspirations.

Customer research can be done in many different ways, however it can be time consuming and resource intensive depending on the type of user you will be approaching. Analyzing your customers social media behavior will give you the opportunity to empathize with your potential target market while discovering valuable insights about them.

Gather information about your potential users and clients by going through their social media profiles.

Look through a person profile and check for her online activity (posts, comments, likes and followers) as well as frequency and level of engagement on different social networks.

Collect relevant information to identify trends and patterns that emerge based on her personal beliefs; the things and people that inspire and influence her; the content that entertains her; and the products/brands and causes she endorses and shares.

Repeat this exercise with at least 10 profiles. Keep in mind that your customer (the one who pays) might be different from the actual user of your idea. Consider both profiles when gathering information.

 **TIPS**

Look for people beyond your personal networks and keep in mind that you might end on a rabbit hole while looking trough people's profiles and their online activity. Focus on one person at a time.

PROFILE

BELIEFS

INSPIRATION

ENTERTAINMENT

SHARE

OBSERVATION LOG

Watching how someone performs a task, uses as service or interacts with a product will allow you to gather insights on how to improve their experiences and provide you with inspiration for innovation.

When asked, people tend to say what they think you want to hear, observing people is an opportunity to learn more about them, why and how they do what they do, while identifying the challenges they face on their daily life.

Observe potential customers and users as they perform day-to-day activities relevant to your idea.

Ask for permission to follow people through parts of their day, or to a store manager to observe people in their space.

Ask the person to do things as they would, if you were not there and describe what you are seeing in detail as it is happening.

Use pictures, videos and notes to record the activity or task the person is doing; her profile; the environment and context she is at; the people, products and services she interacts with; and the insights you get from this observation.

Repeat this exercise observing different people doing the same activity.

 **TIPS**

Look for unexpected reactions and workarounds your potential customer does in order to perform the task.

Describing what you see, instead of interpreting it, is the most important thing to keep in mind while observing.

ACTIVITY

USER PROFILE

ENVIRONMENT

INTERACTION

INSIGHTS

Customer Profile

Customer profiles are realistic representations of people whom your idea will be targeting and share common interests, habits, motivations, needs, etc.

These profiles will help you visualize and empathize with your target audience, making it easier to include their needs, aspirations and goals as the center of your design process to make your idea more appealing to the market.

Gather all the information you have collected from your research and identify patterns among your potential customers to create a realistic profile of a potential customer or user.

Start by giving your profile an identity and context: name, age, gender, location and occupation, and the economic, social and cultural aspects of her life.

Identify the real needs and challenges your customer faces; the tradeoffs of using alternative solutions, and the limitations preventing her to achieve her goals.

Followed by the motivations to buy and try new products and services; her aspirations and the benefits from achieving her goals.

 **TIPS**

Be visual: add drawings and pictures to help you visualize your customer profile.

Your profile should represent a person. Avoid using general information (e.g.: 20 – 30 years old)

CUSTOMER	EXTREME CUSTOMER	EARLY ADOPTER
IDENTITY AND CONTEXT	**IDENTITY AND CONTEXT**	**IDENTITY AND CONTEXT**
NEEDS AND LIMITATIONS	**NEEDS AND LIMITATIONS**	**NEEDS AND LIMITATIONS**
MOTIVATIONS AND ASPIRATIONS	**MOTIVATIONS AND ASPIRATIONS**	**MOTIVATIONS AND ASPIRATIONS**

Business Customer Profile

When you are selling your product or service to another company (business to business model - B2B), you need to profile them, but also get to know and empathize with two particular roles within the organization: the buyer, the person who will be in charge on making the decision (and the risk) of purchasing your product or service; and the user, the one from whom you are creating value.

Familiarize yourself with the companies that are part of your target, their decision making process and the organizational culture.

Start by profiling the companies, their industry and sector, what challenges are they facing and any emerging trends relevant to your offer; and who are their customers and what they are offering to them.

Identify the buyers of your target firms, analyze their personal context, and understand how do they make their procurement decisions, any potential risks associated with buying from you, and what is the most important challenge they face.

Empathize with the users, the environment in which they will be using your product and service, and how can you help them work better.

 **TIPS**

Be visual: add drawings and pictures to help you visualize your business customer profile.

Your profile should represent a realistic company and its employees. Avoid using general information (e.g.: Small and medium enterprise)

COMPANY	BUYER	USER
IDENTITY AND CONTEXT	PERSONAL CONTEXT	PERSONAL CONTEXT
INDUSTRY CHALLENGES AND TRENDS	DECISION MAKING PROCESS AND RISKS OF PURCHASING	WORK ENVIRONMENT
CUSTOMER BASE	CHALLENGES AND NEEDS	EASE OF DOING BUSINESS

JOBS TO BE DONE

The Jobs-to-be-done framework is based on the premise that people hire products and services to get a job done. Focusing on the jobs that your customer segments are trying to solve will allow you to uncover hidden opportunities for innovation and business development.

To fully understand a job to be done and its implications in your customer behavior, it is necessary to consider its functional, emotional and social component, as well as the desired outcome of your customer once the job is done.

Based on your customer and user, create a list of the jobs to be done and select the most important one and relevant for your idea.

Start by analyzing in depth the problem to get a holistic view of the problem, your customer behavior and identify any potential business opportunity.

Describe the fictional component of the job: the specific task your customer wants to achieve; the emotional component: how your customer wants to feel; and the social component: how your customer wants to be perceived by others.

Followed by how the customer will measure success after getting a job done.

 **TIPS**

Write your customer's problem in a sentence starting with an action verb, an object of action, and context. E.g.: 'Eat healthy lunch at school'

DESIRED OUTCOME

SOCIAL COMPONENT

EMOTIONAL COMPONENT

FUNCTIONAL COMPONENT

CUSTOMER PROBLEM

INDUSTRY
RESEARCH

SUBSTITUTES ARE ALWAYS PRESENT, BUT THEY ARE EASY TO OVERLOOK BECAUSE THEY MAY APPEAR TO BE VERY DIFFERENT FROM THE INDUSTRY'S PRODUCT

– MICHAEL E. PORTER

Industry Snapshot

Understanding and knowing the industry and market you will be part of will help you develop your strategy for entering and penetrate it.

An industry analysis provides you with the right information and insights to know if your idea will work, if could be profitable and sustainable, your competitors and their business models, as well as, any potential opportunities for growth, or any barriers or challenges you will face when entering it.

An industry snapshot is an overview of the key and relevant information regarding your industry and its operational context.

The global competitiveness context: including the market conditions at the macroeconomic level, and the economic growth and development of the selected geographical context.

The sustainability progress: the industry progress towards achieving the Sustainable Development Goals (SDGs).

The global risk landscape: the challenges and risks currently facing the world and their implications for your industry.

Ease of doing business: the regulatory environment, infrastructure and capital market conditions that facilitate the starting and operation of a local firm.

TIPS

Review business and market research reports from consulting and market research firms. Be aware that some of this reports are very expensive, however you can get information by looking at reliable news and blog posts quoting them.

GLOBAL COMPETITIVENESS CONTEXT

SUSTAINABILITY PROGRESS

GLOBAL RISK LANDSCAPE

EASE OF DOING BUSINESS

TREND RADAR

Changes in technology, the socio-economical and environmental context, and disruptive events are drivers for trends at the global, regional and local scales, that are followed by consumers changing and adapting their behavior, expectations and attitudes according to them; or by businesses to develop new strategies and innovative products and services.

Visualize the most relevant trends for your industry based on the impact they have.

Social and cultural trends have a direct influence in peoples lives shaping the way a society and its culture evolves.

Business and industry trends outline major changes that will drive disruption, innovative business models and new industry standards.

Technology and new developments are enablers for industry transformation and new consumer experiences.

Categorize the trends accordingly, and prioritize them based on how fast can you apply those trends.

 **TIPS**

Do not go too much in detail when analyzing the trends at this stage. Focusing on understanding the impact it could have on your business.

Revise and update the radar at least once a year.

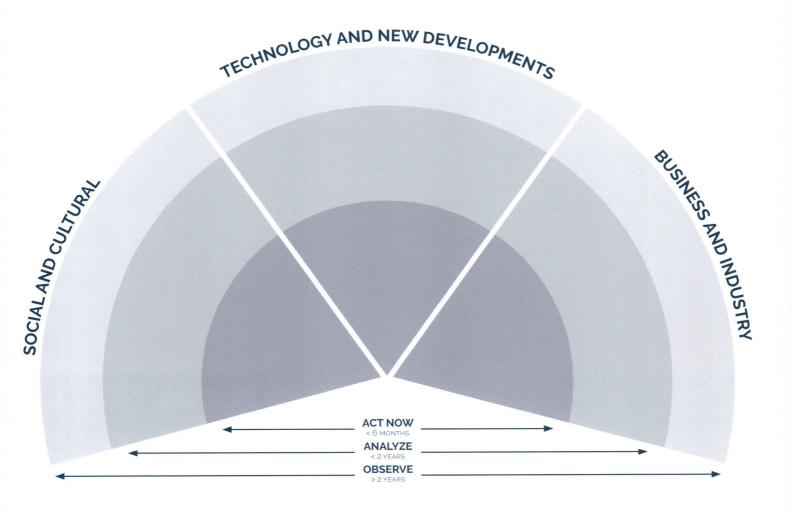

SOCIAL AND CULTURAL

TECHNOLOGY AND NEW DEVELOPMENTS

BUSINESS AND INDUSTRY

ACT NOW
< 6 MONTHS

ANALYZE
< 2 YEARS

OBSERVE
> 2 YEARS

TREND ANALYSIS

An in-depth analysis of trends will help you not only to understand your consumers better, but also a good way to gather insights and inspiration from your competitors, the industry and markets to help you develop a growth strategy for your idea.

Analyze emerging trends that are changing your industry.

Start by looking for the applications of the trends and how businesses and organizations are using them.

Understand the political, socio-economic and technological factors that are driving this trend.

The impact this trend is having in your customer's behavior, needs and desires and the new expectations is creating.

Identify the key takeaways from this trend and ask yourself how can you use this trend to serve your customers better.

 **TIPS**

To gain as wide a perspective as possible, look specifically at other industries, other regions or cultures, or other types of business (e.g. corporate versus start ups).

TREND

APPLICATIONS

IMPACT

INSIGHTS

HOW CAN THIS TREND HELP YOU SERVE YOUR CUSTOMER'S EXPECTATIONS?

COMPETITIVE INTELLIGENCE

One of the most common mistakes entrepreneurs make is to overlook and undervalue their direct competitors, the threats that represent new entrants and the value substitutes provide to your prospective consumers.

A systemic approach to uncover your competitors' current and future strategies by collecting and analyzing information about them will help you make the right decisions to make your business idea more competitive.

Understand your competitors' strategy, behavior and value proposition in order to identify their strengths and weaknesses, and identify your own competitive opportunities.

Identify all the competitors, new entrants and alternatives products and services that your consumers use to address their jobs-to-be-done.

Prioritize and choose the most relevant ones and collect all the information available for them.

Categorize the information regarding the company's profile, its product and services, target market, resources and competences and its value chain.

 **TIPS**

Gather as much information as possible from different sources (including websites, industry reports and databases.

Use competitors products and services so you can experience their business first hand.

MAIN COMPETITOR	NEW ENTRANT	SUBSTITUTES/ALTERNATIVES
PROFILE	**PROFILE**	**PROFILE**
PRODUCT/SERVICE	**PRODUCT/SERVICE**	**PRODUCT/SERVICE**
TARGET MARKET	**TARGET MARKET**	**TARGET MARKET**
RESOURCES AND COMPETENCES	**RESOURCES AND COMPETENCES**	**RESOURCES AND COMPETENCES**
VALUE CHAIN	**VALUE CHAIN**	**VALUE CHAIN**

COMPETITIVE SCOPE

Designing your competitive advantage implies benchmarking with incumbents (currents competitors) and potential new entrants like you, as well as pointing out how you are going to make your offer unique both in terms of assets, resources and competences you want to leverage and in terms of positioning in the competitive scope.

The concept of competitive scope developed by Michael E. Porter is defined as a function of a number of dimensions: geographical scope, industry scope, segment scope, product scope and vertical scope.

A unique positioning in the competitive scope, i.e. where there are no competitors already covering that part of the scope may result in a competitive advantage.

Identify your competitive scope vis-à-vis the one of your competitors.

First, rate your competitors for each one of the 5 dimensions of the competitive scope from 0 (low) at the center to 5 (high).

Connect the dots to create a radar type graph.

Using a different color, repeat the exercise for each competitor.

Then, using a different color again, repeat the exercise for your business paying attention on how to not fully overlay with competitors' scope.

Competitive scope can be narrow or wide. In the case of being narrow, your business will be positioned in a niche. This way result in a competitive advantage that pays attention to the sustainability of the niche in time. In the case of being wide, your business will seek to reach a wider market with a blurred competitive advantage.

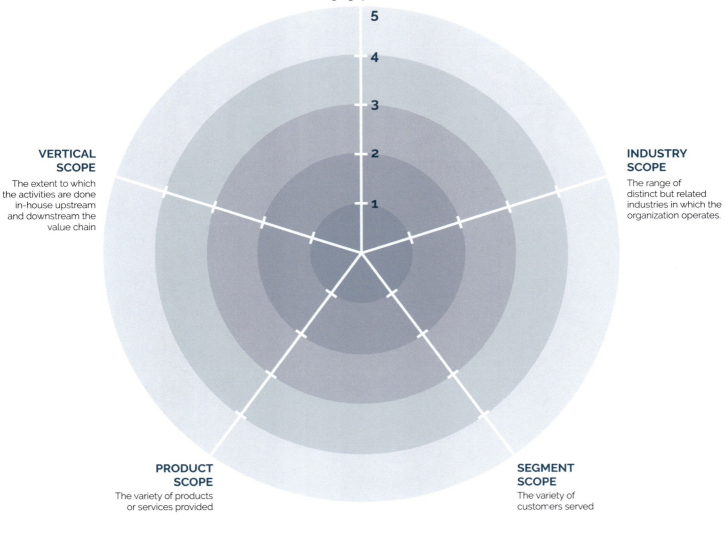

GEOGRAPHIC SCOPE
The number of geographical markets served

VERTICAL SCOPE
The extent to which the activities are done in-house upstream and downstream the value chain

INDUSTRY SCOPE
The range of distinct but related industries in which the organization operates.

PRODUCT SCOPE
The variety of products or services provided

SEGMENT SCOPE
The variety of customers served

Value
PROPOSITION

I BELIEVE SO MUCH IN THE POWER OF PERFORMANCE I DON'T WANT TO CONVINCE PEOPLE. I WANT THEM TO EXPERIENCE IT AND COME AWAY CONVINCED ON THEIR OWN.

– Marina Abramovic

THE ELEMENTS OF VALUE

When a customer is buying your product or service she is not only considering the price, but also what value will she get from using it. That value is perceived by how a product or service that satisfy her functional, emotional and social needs.

Business to Consumer (B2C) Pyramid

Bain & Co. analyzed the most valuable attributes for consumers that could help firms innovate, identify opportunities for growth and deliver a better offer to their consumers, while increasing their loyalty.

SOCIAL

SELF-TRANSCENDENCE

DESIGN / AESTHETICS

BADGE VALUE

FUN / ENTERTAINMENT

HEIRLOOM

AFFILIATION AND BELONGING

EMOTIONAL

REDUCES ANXIETY

REWARDS ME

NOSTALGIA

PROVIDES HOPE

SELF-ACTUALIZATION

WELLNESS

THERAPEUTIC VALUE

MOTIVATION

ATTRACTIVENESS

PROVIDES ACCESS

FUNCTIONAL

SAVES TIMES

SIMPLIFIES

MAKES MONEY

REDUCES RISK

ORGANIZES

INTEGRATES

CONNECTS

REDUCES EFFORT

AVOIDS HASSLES

REDUCES COST

QUALITY

VARIETY

SENSORY APPEAL

INFORMS

Business to Business (B2B) Pyramid

Similar to the B2C pyramid, the B2B pyramid analyzes the 40 fundamental elements of value for B2B buyers, and divides them into five categories, with those providing more objective value at the base, and those that offer more subjective and personal value higher up.

INSPIRATIONAL VALUE

VISION

HOPE · SOCIAL RESPONSIBILITY

INDIVIDUAL VALUE

NETWORK EXPANSION · MARKETABILITY · REPUTATIONAL ASSURANCE

DESIGN / AESTHETICS · GROWTH & DEVELOPMENT · REDUCE ANXIETY · FUN & PERKS

EASE OF DOING BUSINESS

TIME SAVINGS · REDUCE EFFORT · AVAILABILITY · RESPONSIVENESS · EXPERTISE

DECREASE HASSLES · INFORMATION · TRANSPARENCY · VARIETY · COMMITMENT · STABILITY · CULTURAL FIT

CONNECTION · INTEGRATION · ORGANIZATION · SIMPLIFICATION · CONFIGURABILITY · FLEXIBILITY · COMPONENT QUALITY · RISK REDUCTION · REACH

FUNCTIONAL VALUE

IMPROVE TOP LINE · COST REDUCTION · PRODUCT QUALITY · SCALABILITY · INNOVATION

TABLE STAKES

MEETING SPECIFICATIONS · ACCEPTABLE PRICE · REGULATORY COMPLIANCE · ETHICAL STANDARDS

CRITICAL SUCCESS FACTORS

Critical Success Factors are the key elements of value necessary for ensuring the success to your idea within the selected market. Analyze both the market demand and the supply side of your industry in order to identify the most Critical Success Factors that will allow you an advantage over your competitors and satisfy the most important of your customer needs.

Critical Success Factors are always a limited number (usually between 3 to 5) of market needs that are critical for you to fully satisfy your market and that you master *vis-à-vis* your competitors, offering your market more factors than the ones that are critical may result in value that the market is not willing to pay; offering less factors than those that are critical may result at least in conforming to competitors' offer as to be trivial.

Identify the most critical factors that will you an advantage in the industry.

Identify and prioritize the most important elements of value for your consumers.

Evaluate how your competitors are satisfying those needs to your consumers.

Those elements that do not provide much value to your users are either not required or should not be a priority for you.

The elements that act as enablers are the ones that you need to have in order to survive the competition.

Your main priority are the elements that are considered of a high value for your users but are not served by the competition.

 TIPS

Make sure you have completed the Costumer Profiles, Jobs-to-be-Done and Competitive Intelligence exercises combined with the Elements of Value framework, before defining your Critical Success Factors.

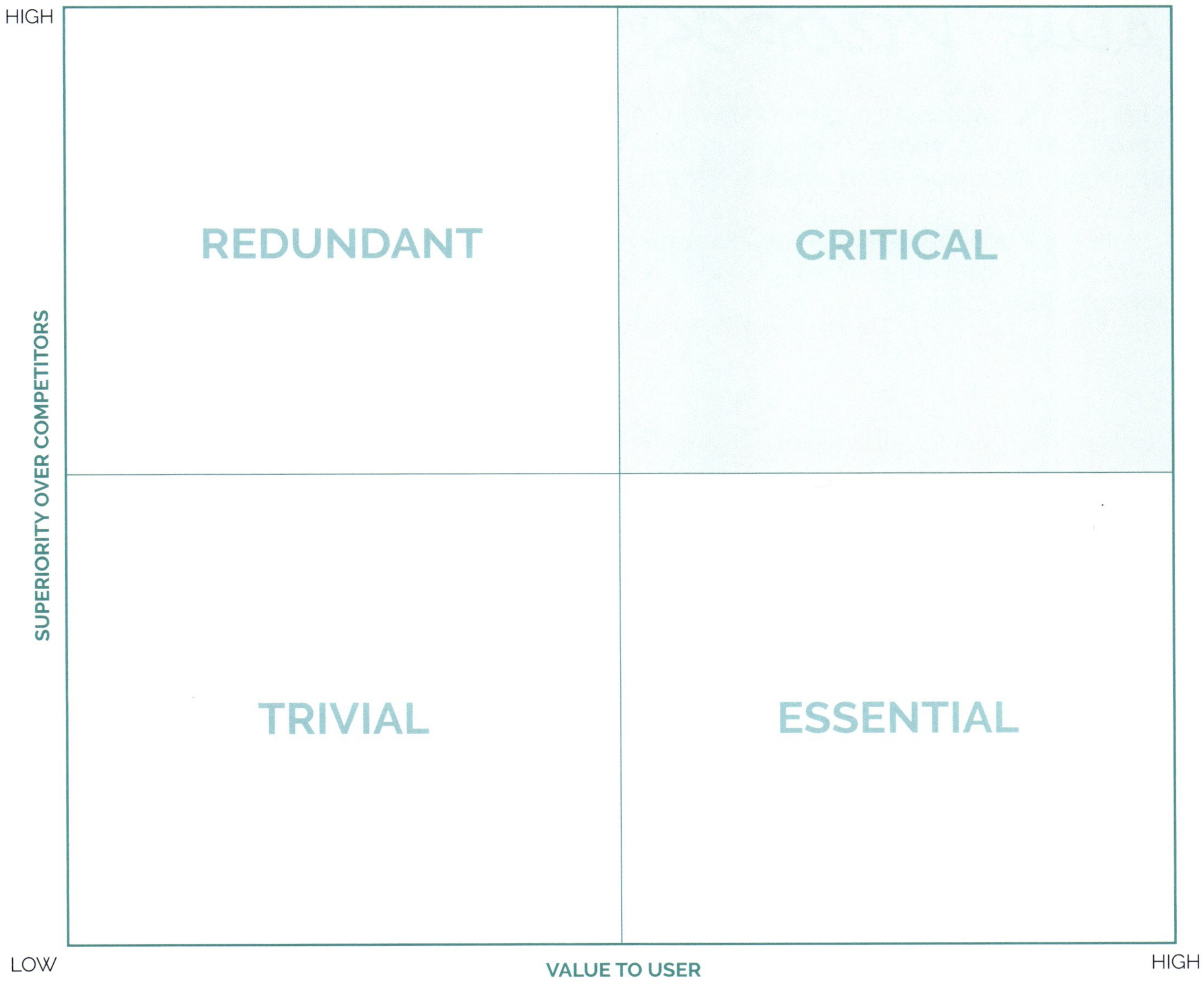
HIGH
REDUNDANT
CRITICAL
SUPERIORITY OVER COMPETITORS
TRIVIAL
ESSENTIAL
LOW
VALUE TO USER
HIGH

Value Proposition Concept

The products, services and experiences you offer to your customer are intended to create value for them. Use the elements of value framework to create a solution that helps your customers address their jobs-to-be-done while generating value for them.

You might have noticed that your idea keeps evolving over time. A good way to make sure the core and more critical elements of your idea remain as part of your designed solution is creating a value proposition concept.

To better visualize and communicate your idea, imagine it as it was in a box on a supermarket shelf.

Start by understanding the benefits and elements of value that you want to deliver to your customers.

Describe the key features that your products and services will have that will allow you to deliver the value.

Finalize your concept, by describing the components and how complex they can be to generate or manufacture.

Identify any potential doubts or challenges you may face or the key elements that validate your idea.

 **TIPS**

Your solution does not need to be perfect, but make sure it helps your customers to satisfy their needs and solve their problems, is feasible and can be sold to make a profit.

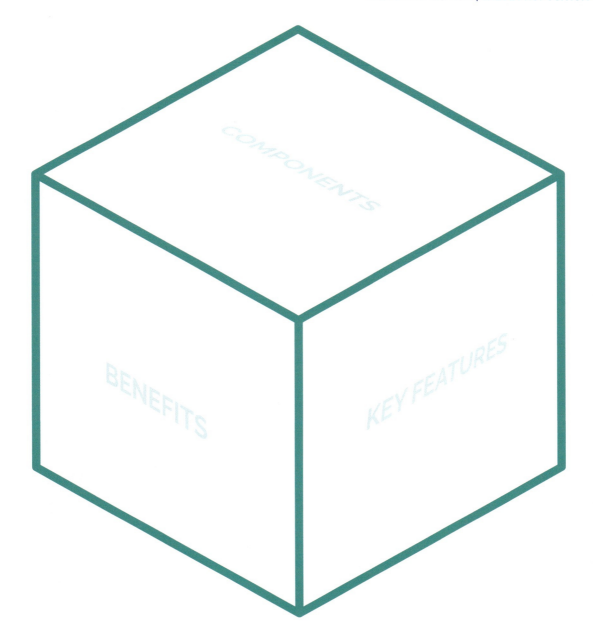

Value Proposition Design

There are different ways to help your customer achieve their goals, satisfy their needs and create value for them. Forcing yourself to create at least 6 different variations of your current value proposition will help you to identify opportunities to design a winning value proposition.

A well-designed value proposition focuses on addressing the critical success factors while delivering specific benefits to the consumers; its unique features can be produced with the available technology and materials, can be sold at a competitive price and has a potential market willing to buy it.

Improve your value proposition concept by generating new ones.

Analyze each one of your value proposition elements: components and its functionality, key features and benefits.

From those elements identify the ones you can eliminate.

Are there any elements that you can insert to make your value proposition more appealing?

Raise or reduce the number of elements to make your value proposition more competitive within your industry.

Can you bundle your value proposition elements with other elements? Or can you unbundle them to make new ones?

 TIPS

The goal is to generate as many ideas as you can, no matter if they seem unrealistic or not feasible at the beginning, you can refine them later.

Feel free to use any creative or brainstorm exercise to help you generate ideas.

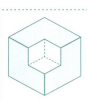 ELIMINATE

 INSERT

 RAISE

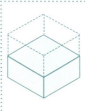 REDUCE

 BUNDLE

 UNBUNDLE

EXPERIENCE JOURNEY

Developing a product or a service is not just about the product or service itself, but also about the whole experience your customers and users will have while interacting with your company.

This includes how they will find out about you, how and where they will purchase your products, how they will use them and how they will keep using it in the future. An experience journey map allows you to visualize different scenarios of a customer experience from beginning to end, helping you improve your strategy to deliver more value to them.

Create a visual map of all the steps your customer will follow to interact with your company, before, during and after purchasing your products and services.

Define the main touchpoints, the points of contact with your business, and the channels you will use to provide them (products, website, ads, stores, call centers, etc.)

Understand what will motivate your customer to keep going to the next stage and what emotions do you want them to feel.

Design the best experience possible to match the emotions and ensure your customer engagement.

TIPS

This is as a step-by-step journey of your customer interacting with your company, adapt the tool according to your own needs.

EXPERIENCE

MOTIVATION

CHANNEL

TOUCHPOINT

BEFORE PURCHASE

AFTER PURCHASE

DURING PURCHASE

Market
VALIDATION

IF YOU ARE NOT
EMBARRASSED BY THE FIRST
VERSION OF YOUR PRODUCT,
YOU'VE LAUNCHED TOO LATE.

— REID HOFFMAN

VALIDATION TEST PLAN

As you move forward with your business idea it is important to validate it and learn how it will work and be perceived in the market.

Until now, all you have is an idea and assumptions on how that idea could work. You might have validated some of them with experts but is the real customer and users who will give you the right insights to continue this journey. Having a clear plan on how to test those hypotheses will save you time and keep your learning process updated.

Develop a plan to test and validate your ideas in the market.

Make a list of all the assumptions and hypotheses you have made so far, these can be regarding the problems and jobs to be done you are addressing; your solution and its features; and the business model and pricing strategies.

Prioritize on the aspects that are more uncertain to develop a fast-paced test plan to gather valuable insights to improve your value proposition and your business model as your move forward.

Repeat this exercise every time you want to validate an idea or a hypothesis.

TIPS

HYPOTHESES

TEST

METRICS

RESULTS

NEXT STEPS

INSIGHTS

USER TEST STORYBOARD

Building a prototype without a clear understanding on what are the elements should have or how is it going to be used, could delay the execution of your validation plan and hinder your learning process.

A user test storyboard along with an idea test plan will guide your rapid prototype building process as well as your user test performance. Repeating this process, as you move forward for all your hypothesis will get you closer to a better suitable product or service for the market.

Create a storyboard to visualize your validation test.

Using between 10 to 15 frames, illustrate each stage of your validation test.

Start on the box on the top left. This frame will set the context for your test and allow the user to experience your business for the first time.

Add enough details to each frame to help you identify the resources you need to incorporate in your prototype.

Resist to incorporate new ideas or features into your test. Use your validation test plan to guide your storyboard.

Keep your test short and concise. A usability test should not last longer than 30 minutes.

TIPS

For a more detailed storyboard use a sheet of paper for each frame.

Make sure you have all the information in your storyboard before you start building your prototype.

RAPID PROTOTYPING GUIDE

A rapid prototype is a fast and cheap way to validate your ideas and hypotheses. Everything can be prototyped to simulate the real feel of your product or service to gather feedback from users.

There are many different ways to do a prototype; the following is a curated guide of tools for rapid prototyping that can be done in less than a day and can be done without spending that much money.

Design and develop a rapid prototype to validate your idea.

Choose a hypothesis you want to validate from your idea test plan and identify the type of prototype you want to build depending on your idea.

Create your user test storyboard and then build your prototype.

Use the right tools to create your prototype:

For physical products: 3D printing, cardboard and any other construction materials, and CAD software.

For screen based: Keynote or PowerPoint, Wordpress, Squarespace, InVision and Sketch.

For paper based: Keynote, PowerPoint, Canva and the Adobe Suite.

 **TIPS**

Use this guide combined with the idea test plan and user test storyboard tools.

Your prototype does not need to be perfect, but should be good enough and look as real as possible to showcase the idea and how it works.

PROOF ON CONCEPT

A early model prototype version of your product or service that helps you validate the concept behind your idea and test

VISUAL PROTOTYPE

A visual representation of your product that represents either the real size of a scale version of the physical appearance of your product.

WORKING PROTOTYPE

A working version of your product that allows user to try and test its functionalities

WIREFRAME

A simple visual guide using only lines and boxes to represent how the elements of a website, software or an app are distributed on the screen, the prioritization of the content and the intended functionality and user interaction flow.

INTERACTIVE

An interactive version of a website, software or an app that looks and functions just as the real one. There are several platforms that allow you to design digital products and create comprehensive interactive prototypes.

VIDEO

A video prototype explaining how a product or a service works. It can show a whole user experience journey or specific features and functionalities depending on the test plan.

ROLE PLAY

Recreate how a user experiences a service or interacts with a product by making the situation as real as possible.

MARKETING MATERIAL

Newsletters campaigns, online ads and any other marketing materials that represent how will you sell your product or services and show your users its main benefits and test their willingness and ability to test.

SPACE

A scale or real size model of the architecture, element distribution and interior design of a physical space.

BUSINESS
MODELING

A BUSINESS MODEL DESCRIBES HOW YOUR COMPANY CREATES, DELIVERS AND CAPTURES VALUE.

– STEVE BLANK

Culture Moodboard

Creating the right culture for your business will help you achieve your goals and deliver the right image to the market while keeping your team motivated. Organizational culture is shaped by your company values and identity, your employees and their interactions and how is your business perceived in the market.

An organization culture mood-board is a visual tool to help you visualize and represent the culture you want to experience within your company or team.

Create a visual collage that represents the main elements of your team culture.

Use an empty wall or a white-board as the space for your physical mood-board.

Collect images, texts and objects that represent the symbols, stories, rituals and events that will be experienced at your company; the behavior and emotions of your employees; and how you want to be perceived by your customers and other external stakeholders

Choose the most important ones and arrange your images on the board according to each category. Reflect and select the ones that you will use as inspiration for the following session.

TIPS

Be visual. Do not do this exercise in a computer, use magazines and printed images to show your ideas.

Use this exercise with your team, to make sure everyone's point of view and aspirations are represented.

SYMBOLS

RITUALS

EVENTS

EMOTIONS

VALUES

STORIES

STRUCTURE

EXPERIENCES

OUTSIDE PERCEPTION

Business DNA

Your Business unique DNA is the "genetic code" of your business and will shape the way your company operates, communicate and interact with all the stakeholders.

Having a clear and define DNA is what makes your business unique, and will guide you to develop your strategies and stand out from your competitors.

Define your business DNA.

Start by defining what are your business or team core values.

Define your mission statement: what your business do, consider your competitive advantage, target market and value proposition.

Vision: your goals for the future, the contribution you strive to achieve within your industry and the impact your company has on the stakeholders and the world as a whole.

Strategic orientation: which set of actions will your organization follow to reach its goals.

Reflect and iterate them until they 'feel right' and your whole team feels like represent them.

TIPS

Remember your business DNA is alive and continuously evolves in time and should be communicated through-out the company.

VALUES

MISSION

VISION

STRATEGIC ORIENTATION

BUSINESS MODEL

There are many definitions out there of what a business model is, one of the simplest way to put it, is how you will make money while creating value to your stakeholders.

There are many components to a great business model, including your customer segments, your value proposition and the relationships between them. You have already developed and designed them, creating a visual model of how your business works will help you communicate your idea better and create different scenarios for more innovative model.

Visualize your business model by showcasing the main relationships along the main stakeholders.

First place your company in one of the circles of the chart.

Then add your clients, users, and other stakeholders (suppliers, partners, etc.).

Connect the stakeholders to represent all kind of transactions between your company and stakeholders, monetary (financial and revenue streams), product/service, information and benefits.

 **TIPS**

Keep the number of stakeholders to a maximum of nine.

The lines serve only as a guide. Use arrows to show the flow direction and feel free to create your own lines.

ORGANIZATIONAL STRUCTURE

In order to get the things done, and thrive in the marketplace you need to make sure everyone in your organization knows their role, their responsibilities and how they relate to other main stakeholders.

Each organization is different, and although there are some popular organizational structures, is up to you to design a structure that reflects your values and will allow your business culture to develop. Look for a balance of power, responsibilities and communication between roles and make sure it will improve productivity and efficiency.

Design and visualize your organization management and operation structure.

Start by placing the founder team members first.

Then add employees, collaborators and board members as you expect them to interact with each others as the company grows.

Create different scenarios until you find the right structure that matches your business culture and DNA.

TIPS

Before you start take a look at some organizational structures from your competitors or organizations you admire.

Key Business Processes

The key processes are the most important set of tasks and activities that must exist for your business to function properly, having a maximum impact on the success of it. Having a clear understanding of your key business processes will facilitate the implementation of your business model.

The processes can be divided into three main categories: build, operate and deliver.

Analyze your key business processes and identify opportunities for improvement.

List and prioritize all the relevant activities and processes you need to perform in order to build your product, operate your business and deliver value to your customers.

Identify the cost, control or differentiation drivers for each one of the key business processes and the linkages between them.

Identify or create opportunities for reducing costs, differentiate your offer, or gain control over an asset, and develop the feasible strategies to achieve them.

 **TIPS**

Make a detailed list of your tasks and activities, then focus on the ones that have the most impact on your business.

BUILD　　　　　　**KEY DRIVER**　　　　　　　　　**OPPORTUNITY**

OPERATE

DELIVER

RESOURCES AND COMPETENCES

Your resources are the factors and elements that you posses and can be transformed into products and services through your key business processes. Your competences is how your business manages its resources to function.

Resources can be divided in three main categories: tangible: physical (plant, equipment, real state) or financial (capital, borrowing capacity); intangible: Technology (patents, copyrights, trade secrets, licenses; reputation (brands, relationships) or culture; and human: knowledge and know-how, capability to interact and communicate, or motivation.

Competences can be divided into process (innovation, market penetration); or function (marketing, research and development, production, etc)

Identify the key resources and competences required to make your business work.

First list of all your resources and competences, classifying them according to the form.

Then underline only those that you believe are key, unique assets to deliver appropriate value to your prospect customers.

TIPS

Your key resources, and only them, will be used later on to check the fit among your business model building blocks.

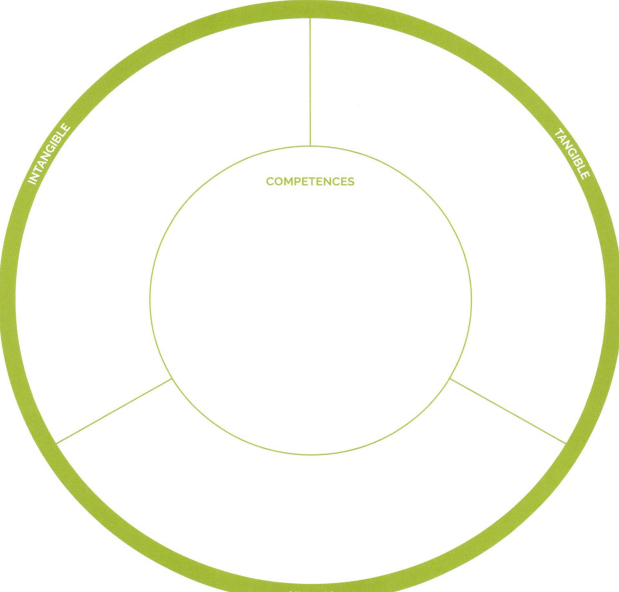

COMPETENCES

INTANGIBLE

TANGIBLE

HUMAN

COMPETITIVE ADVANTAGE

The concept of competitive advantage developed by Michael E. Porter is a superiority that a firm has over its rivals that creates greater profits.

There are two main ways in which a business can achieve a competitive advantage over its rivals: cost advantage (when a business provides the same products and services as its competitors, albeit at a lower cost) and differentiation (when a business provides better products and services as its competitors). The two may be combined.

To work on your competitors advantage you might consider to identify its roots, taking a resource-based approach as suggested by Robert M. Grant.

Define your competitive advantage by assessing your resources and competences.

Analyze your resources and competences and identify the key ones that allow you to:

Establish a competitive advantage by creating value for customers (relevant;) or if is not widely available within the industry (scarcity).

Sustain that competitive advantage, by its ability to support a competitive advantage over the long term (durability); not easily transferred between firms (transferability) or to be copied by competitors (replicability)

Appropriate the returns from the competitive advantage, according to who owns them (proprietary rights); the division of returns between the firm and its members (bargain power); and dependence on corporate systems and reputation (embeddedness).

ⓘ TIPS

At the beginning of your entrepreneurial journey focus on the resources and competences that will allow you to gain a competitive advantage.

ESTABLISHING A COMPETITIVE ADVANTAGE

RELEVANCE

SCARCITY

SUSTAINING A COMPETITIVE ADVANTAGE

DURABILITY

TRANSFERABILITY

REPLICABILITY

APPROPRIATING A COMPETITIVE ADVANTAGE

PROPERTY RIGHTS

BARGAINING POWER

EMBEDDEDNESS

BUSINESS MODEL ALIGNMENT

Alignment and fit of your business model building blocks are essential for success. This means that critical success factors, experienced by your target market, should be aligned with the features of your product or service offer's competitive advantage, that again is the direct result of how well you built and leveraged on your key resources and competences.

All the three building blocks of a business model have to fit together to check for a basic business model alignment.

Design and visualize your business model building blocks and check for alignment.

Start by transcribing your critical success factors, competitive advantage and resources and competences respectively from previous exercises.

Then check that the three building blocks fit on each others. To that you must ask yourself:

What is critical for my target market?

Is my product or service offer aligning exactly to those critical needs from the market? Is it doing this better than all my competitors?

What kind of resources and competences do I need to support that competitive advantage? Are those the one that I have?

 **TIPS**

Use this exercise with your team to discuss about the fit among the building blocks of your business model.

In case of mis-alignment reconsider the building block going back to previous exercises.

Reiterate the process several times until you find a perfect fit.

CRITICAL SUCCESS
FACTORS

COMPETITIVE
ADVANTAGE

RESOURCES
AND COMPETENCES

MARKET SIZE

You have already identified a potential customer who need your product or service, now you need to ensure there are enough potential customers to be able to turn your idea into a sustainable business.

Analyze your market and define how many customers need your products or services.

Start with the total available market (TAM) for your product or service. That is how big is the universe.

Estimate the number of customers that can be fulfilled or served by all businesses that offer a particular solution, product, or service; that is your served available market (SAM).

Find some market research or make a best guess on the percentage of those people who have the problem you are solving and will be willing to buy your product or service; or can be reached by your marketing and sales efforts. That is your serviceable obtainable market (SOM).

TIPS

Be realistic about how many customers can you actually reach and serve.

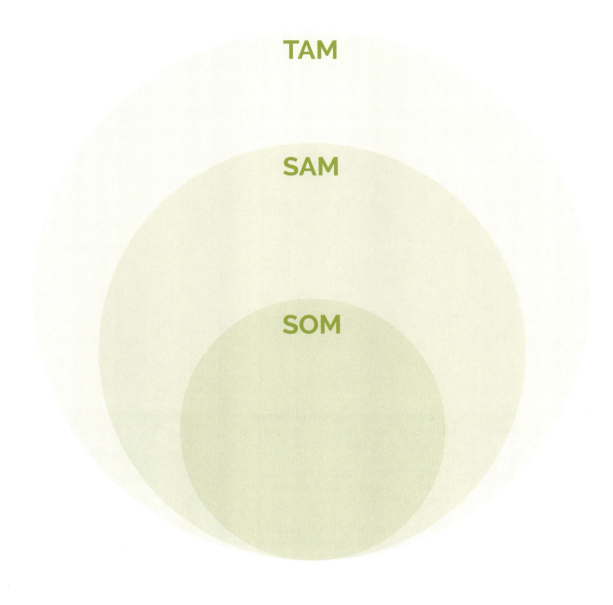

Marketing Plan

Having a good product or offering a great service is not enough, you need to develop the right strategy in order to get noticed by your customers and deliver your value proposition.

A strong marketing plan will guide you to develop the actions and efforts to reach your target market and increase your customer base.

Define a marketing plan to get new customers, increase your revenues and beat your competition.

Set up a clear goal and purpose for your marketing actions, and what customer segments you want to reach.

Elaborate the right message or offer, highlighting your product or service benefits that are meaningful to your audience.

Choose the right medium or channel to deliver your message and create an experience for your customers.

Every marketing effort should have a call to action, to engage your audience an encourage them to make a purchase.

Identify the costs for each one of the activities and identify which one has the best return on investment.

 **TIPS**

It is important that you set realistic and measurable goals, This will help you to track the effectiveness of your marketing messages and activities.

GOAL

AUDIENCE

MESSAGE

MEDIA

CALL TO ACTION

BUDGET

GOAL

AUDIENCE

MESSAGE

MEDIA

CALL TO ACTION

BUDGET

GOAL

AUDIENCE

MESSAGE

MEDIA

CALL TO ACTION

BUDGET

Go to Market Strategy

A go to market strategy is a detailed plan you will follow to reach your target market and deliver your value proposition to them and achieve a competitive advantage. It combines all your efforts to design, develop and improve your value proposition; your marketing activities; and the sales management and post-sales support.

Define the strategy to launch your product on the market and a 3 years roadmap for growth.

Define your product strategy and how it will evolve over time, the marketing efforts to engage customers and reach new markets, and the sales channels and the activities for building and managing your customer relationships.

Create a timeline to map your goals for the next 3 years and the efforts you will have to make in order to achieve them.

TIPS

Be realistic with your plan and set goals that you can achieve considering your resources and competences.

VALUE PROPOSITION

MARKETING

SALES AND SUPPORT

GOALS

EFFORTS

BRAND
IDENTITY

BRANDING IS ABOUT MAKING
AN EMOTIONAL CONNECTION

— Alina Wheeler

BRAND PERSONALITY

Your brand is how your company will be perceived in the market; you need to make sure that all your brand elements reflect your company culture, DNA and the emotions you want your customers to experience and relate.

Before starting designing your brand elements (name and visual elements) identify what is the personality you want to convey. Your brand will not only help you differentiate from your competitors but also leave a memorable impression.

Develop a brand that will be easy to recognize by your customers and represent your business DNA.

Start by prioritizing your core values and customer segments and keep them in mind while doing this exercise.

Assess your brand personality using the brand archetypes characteristics.

When choosing your archetypes make sure you do not select more than 3; a brand could get lost, if it has a lot of different personality elements.

TIPS

Do not over think this exercise. When choosing your archetypes, keep in mind your customer, the industry, geographical context and your products or services.

KING

In Control

Assertive

WISE

Trustworthy

Intelligent

HERO

Adventurous

Brave

REBEL

Rebellious

Outrageous

SEDUCTRESS

Desirable

Sexy

JOKER

Fun

Playful

DREAMER

Idealistic

Creative

MAIDEN

Innocent

Kind

FRIEND

Straightforward

Sociable

MOTHER

Generous

Caring

Name Generation

One of the main elements people remember about a company or a product is its name. Your name should represent your brand personality, be easy to say, positive and timeless.

Choosing a name could be very overwhelming, and you should not rush it and take some time reflecting on the selected name before making it official. Your company name should be original and distinctive from the competition within your industry, verify that is available not only online but also check for trademarks.

Use your brand personality to brainstorm a name that represents it.

Choose at least 5 different themes or categories to help you structure your brainstorming session.

Generate different names and word associations for each of the categories. You don't have to do this in an specific order, but fill in the categories as they come to your mind.

Choose the one that stand out the most and really represents you, then check the availability of your selected name.

TIPS

Use a website like namechk.com or namecheckr.com to validate the availability of your selected name.

Theme 1	Theme 2	Theme 3	Theme 4	Theme 5

NAME AVAILABILITY

Domain

Social media handles:

VISUAL ELEMENTS

Usually when people think of a brand, they think of a logo. Your brand identity is a mix of different elements, your personality and name, but also the symbols, colors and emotions they transmit to your audience.

These elements will help your brand be more memorable, consistent and attractive while differentiating you from your competitors. A graphic designer is recommended to design your brand but you can develop your brand identity in-house using the resources you have access to.

Choose the visual elements that will represent your brand.

Start by creating a mood-board to envision and visualize your brand elements, using a variety of images of symbols, packaging, context, users, products, etc.

Use the elements of your mood-board as inspiration to sketch, design and test some ideas for your logo, color palette, typography, and the look and feel of your brand.

Select the ones that represent your business and your values the most, remember they should be consistent and immediately recognizable and allow you to stand out from your rivals.

TIPS

Once you have selected your visual elements, print them and see how they look in paper. Keep in mind that color may changes depending on the printer, screen, paper etc.

LOGO

LOOK AND FEEL

COLOR PALETTE

TYPOGRAPHY

Financial
MODEL

NEVER EVER COMPETE ON PRICES, INSTEAD COMPETE ON SERVICES AND INNOVATION.

– JACK MA

 Costs

One of the most important financial exercises an entrepreneur should make is to calculate the costs associated with her business. These include all the expenses necessaries to design and build the product, operate the business, and sale and deliver it to the consumers.

Costs can be variable if they change in proportion to the production of goods or services, these are the ones involved to build and deliver your product or service, including raw materials, packaging, direct labor and distribution); or can be fixed if they remain constant whatever the amount of goods or services produced or sold, these include rent payment and salaries.

Calculate all the associated costs of your business.

Start by creating the list of your key business process and calculate the costs for each one of them.

ⓘ TIPS

Do not forget to include employees salaries (including yours)

COST TO BUILD

COST TO OPERATE

COST TO DELIVER

PRICING

There are different strategies to decide the right price for your product or service that will help you to maximize your profit, so your business can be sustainable over time. Defining the right price is one of the most important business decisions any entrepreneur can make, however there is no single right strategy.

Your ideal strategy allows you to charge more than your costs but less or equal than what your customers are willing to pay, while allowing you to achieve your desired positioning in the market.

Analyze and define the pricing strategy right for your business.

Create different scenarios following the 9 strategies presented.

Cost-led: calculate the total costs and add a margin.
Customer-led: match your customers willingness to pay.
Competition-led: determine your competitors price and decide your pricing.

Introductory offer: discount your product for a limited during its launch phase.
Odd numbers: maximize profit by making micro-adjustments in the price.
Skimming: start with a high price and go down gradually.
Bundled: offer a set of products or services with a perceived high value.
Free or subsidized: offer your product for free or subsidized for a customer segment while getting your revenues from another.
Dynamic pricing: adjust price in response to real-time supply and demand.

 **TIPS**

Don't confuse price (the money your customers pay) with costs (the money it costs to build, operate and deliver your product).

Once you have determined a price, check using the Ballpark Figure tool if it makes sense financially.

CUSTOMER WILLINGNESS TO PAY

PRICE RANGE

CUSTOMER-LED	COMPETITION-LED	DYNAMIC PRICING
ODD NUMBERS	SKIMMING	BUNDLED
COST-LED	INTRODUCTORY OFFER	FREE OR SUBSIDIZED

TOTAL COSTS

BALLPARK FIGURE

A ballpark figure is a rough estimate of your overall financial plan. It will help you to have a sense of the current or future financial state of your business without spending to much time creating a full balance statement.

Roughly estimate your profit over the next 3-5 years.

Define how many units can you sell on an average purchase (average unit sale), the frequency in which your customer buys your product or uses your service (purchase frequency) and the average price (selling price) for it and the number of clients (serviceable obtainable market) who will be buying from you over a period of time. These are your revenues.

Subtract the total cost of your business operations and you will have the rough estimate of your profit.

You can repeat this exercise for a month, a quarter or a year period to create different financial scenarios and validate your assumptions.

TIPS

The goal is to make the right assumptions and gather a sense on how financially sustainable can your business be.

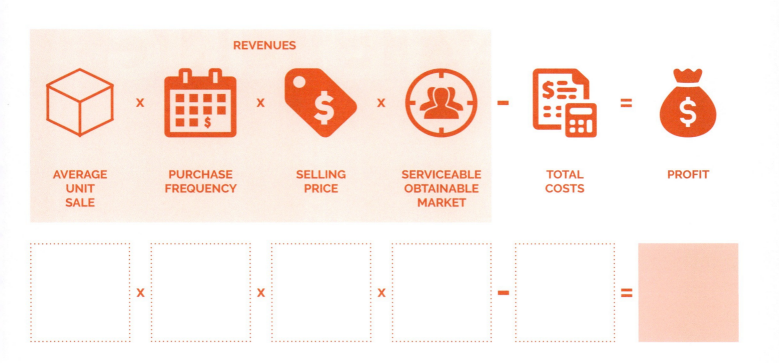

REVENUES

AVERAGE UNIT SALE   x   PURCHASE FREQUENCY   x   SELLING PRICE   x   SERVICEABLE OBTAINABLE MARKET   –   TOTAL COSTS   =   PROFIT

Business
STORYTELLING

PEOPLE DO NOT BUY GOODS AND SERVICES. THEY BUY RELATIONS, STORIES AND MAGIC

– SETH GODIN

STORYTELLING BLUEPRINT

If you want to sell your idea, you need to pitch it. A well delivered pitch starts with the right story; A storytelling blueprint will help you structure and organize all the key elements you need to develop your story: your business, your audience and your strategy behind telling it.

Identify the main components of your narrative to create a powerful story that resonates with your audience and help you achieve your goals.

Know and empathize with your audience, who are they and what do they care about.

Describe the key elements of your business model, who your customers are and what problem are you solving; highlight your product features and benefits.

How, when and where are your going to deliver your story.

Develop a clear strategy for your story, why do you want to deliver it and what would you like to achieve.

 **TIPS**

 **AUDIENCE**

 **BUSINESS MODEL**

 **DELIVERY**

 ASK

Elevator Pitch

The story says that you might encounter a potential investor on an elevator ride, so you only have about 30 seconds to pitch your idea and get the investor's attention. An elevator pitch is a brief, yet effective, summary of your business.

Your elevator pitch should be easily adaptable to your audience or situation, should show your passion for your idea and be memorable.

Create a short but effective pitch of your business that you can share in less than 30 seconds.

Create a storyboard for your elevator pitch, including the goal behind the pitch, and the purpose of your company.

Introduce your customer and the problem you are solving for them.

Once you got the attention, show if possible your solutions and highlight it's uniqueness.

Invite your audience to engage with you and give them the next steps to reach your goal.

Following your storyboard, write down your pitch making sure you are not using more than 200 words and synthesize your elevator pitch in a tweet, using less than 130 characters

 **TIPS**

GOAL

YOUR PURPOSE

PROBLEM

SOLUTION

UNIQUENESS

CALL TO ACTION

YOUR PITCH

TWEET IT

Business Pitch

Create an easy to follow story that will engage your audience and have a positive impact for your business. You probably will not have that much time to explain every single detail about your new business idea, you need to make sure you deliver the right amount of information in the best way possible.

Make your audience follow your pitch as they were reading their favorite book or movie. Practice your storytelling and presentations design skills, and if possible have a prototype to show.

Use your storytelling blueprint and create your pitch storyboard.

Start with short introduction, introduce your customers and the problem you are addressing. Use trends and industry research insights to stress the importance of the problem.

Explain how your solution works and walk the audience through your customer journey using a demo.

Present how your business works and makes money and how are you planning to get customers.

What is your competitive advantage, and your efforts create a barrier to future competition.

Present financials with simple models that are easy to understand and close with your team expertise and call to action.

TIPS

Use a simple language.

If you are using a presentation deck or any other audiovisual aid, be prepared in case something goes wrong.

Prepare in advance answers to any potential questions that your audience might ask.

INTRODUCTION	PROBLEM AND CUSTOMERS	TRENDS AND INSIGHTS	SOLUTION
MARKET	BUSINESS MODEL	MARKETING PLAN	UNIQUENESS
KEY ASSETS	FINANCIAL	TEAM	MILESTONES AND ASK

APPENDIX

Find out more on:

entrepreneurship.design

REFERENCES

BUSINESS DESIGN

CHANGE BY DESIGN: HOW DESIGN THINKING TRANSFORMS ORGANIZATIONS AND INSPIRES INNOVATION
Tim Brown (2009)

SPRINT: HOW TO SOLVE BIG PROBLEMS AND TEST NEW IDEAS IN JUST FIVE DAYS
Jake Knapp, John Zeratsky and Braden Kowitz (2016)

THE DESIGN OF BUSINESS: WHY DESIGN THINKING IS THE NEXT COMPETITIVE ADVANTAGE
Roger L. Martin (2009)

THIS IS SERVICE DESIGN THINKING: BASICS, TOOLS, CASES.
Marc Stickdorn and Jakob Schneider (2012)

BUSINESS MODELING

BUSINESS MODEL GENERATION: A HANDBOOK FOR VISIONARIES, GAME CHANGERS, AND CHALLENGERS
Alexander Osterwalder and Yves Pigneur (2010)

PLATFORM REVOLUTION: HOW NETWORKED MARKETS ARE TRANSFORMING THE ECONOMY AND HOW TO MAKE THEM WORK FOR YOU
Geoffrey G. Parker et al (2017)

REINVENT YOUR BUSINESS MODEL: HOW TO SEIZE THE WHITE SPACE FOR TRANSFORMATIVE GROWTH
Mark W. Johnson (2018)

CREATIVITY

CREATIVE CONFIDENCE: UNLEASHING THE CREATIVE POTENTIAL WITHIN US ALL
Tom Kelley and David Kelley (2013)

MADE TO STICK: WHY SOME IDEAS SURVIVE AND OTHERS DIE
Chip Heath and Dan Heath (2007)

ORIGINALS: HOW NON-CONFORMISTS MOVE THE WORLD
Adam Grant (2017)

STEAL LIKE AN ARTIST: 10 THINGS NOBODY TOLD YOU ABOUT BEING CREATIVE
Austin Kleon (2012)

THE TEN FACES OF INNOVATION: STRATEGIES FOR HEIGHTENING CREATIVITY
Tom Kelley (2016)

WHERE GOOD IDEAS COME FROM: THE NATURAL HISTORY OF INNOVATION
Steven Johnson (2011)

ENTREPRENEURSHIP

THE $100 STARTUP: REINVENT THE WAY YOU MAKE A LIVING, DO WHAT YOU LOVE, AND CREATE A NEW FUTURE
Chris Guillebeau (2012)

THE LEAN STARTUP: HOW TODAY'S ENTREPRENEURS USE CONTINUOUS INNOVATION TO CREATE RADICALLY SUCCESSFUL BUSINESSES
Eric Ries (2011)

THE STARTUP OWNER'S MANUAL: THE STEP-BY-STEP GUIDE FOR BUILDING A GREAT COMPANY
Steve Blank and Bob Dorf (2012)

ZERO TO ONE: NOTE ON START UPS, OR HOW TO BUILD THE FUTURE
Peter Thiel and Blake Masters (2014)

LEADERSHIP

DREAM TEAMS: WORKING TOGETHER WITHOUT FALLING APART
Shane Snow (2018)

INSIGHT: THE SURPRISING TRUTH ABOUT HOW OTHERS SEE US, HOW WE SEE OURSELVES, AND WHY THE ANSWERS MATTER MORE THAN WE THINK
Tasha Eurich (2018)

START WITH WHY: HOW GREAT LEADERS INSPIRE EVERYONE TO TAKE ACTION
Simon Sinek (2009)

MARKETING AND CONSUMER BEHAVIOR

BRAND THINKING AND OTHER NOBLE PURSUITS
Debbie Millman (2013)

DESIGNING BRAND IDENTITY: AN ESSENTIAL GUIDE FOR THE WHOLE BRANDING TEAM
Alina Wheeler (2017)

TREND-DRIVEN INNOVATION: BEAT ACCELERATING CUSTOMER EXPECTATIONS
Henry Manson et al. (2015)

SMALL DATA: THE TINY CLUES THAT UNCOVER HUGE TRENDS.
Martin Lindstrom (2017)

PURPLE COW: TRANSFORM YOUR BUSINESS BY BEING REMARKABLE
Seth Godin (2005)

STORYTELLING

LET THE STORY DO THE WORK: THE ART OF STORYTELLING FOR BUSINESS SUCCESS
Esther K. Choy (2017)

RESONATE: PRESENT VISUAL STORIES THAT TRANSFORM AUDIENCES
Nancy Duarte (2010)

THE BACK OF THE NAPKIN: SOLVING PROBLEMS AND SELLING IDEAS WITH PICTURES
Dan Roam (2008)

THE STORYTELLING ANIMAL: HOW STORIES MAKE US HUMAN
Jonathan Gottschall (2013)

STRATEGY

BLUE OCEAN STRATEGY: HOW TO CREATE UNCONTESTED MARKET SPACE AND MAKE COMPETITION IRRELEVANT
W. Chan Kim and Renee Mauborgne (2005)

CONTEMPORARY STRATEGY ANALYSIS
Robert M. Grant (2016)

JOBS TO BE DONE: THEORY TO PRACTICE
Anthony W. Ulwick (2016)

ON COMPETITION
Michael E. Porter (2008)

THE AUTHORS

MARIO A. VARON

Mario A. Varon is partner of **strategique**.
He is an experienced business designer helping
entrepreneurs develop sustainable business solutions
that can improve people's lives.

He is also the co-founder of socialBaq and a member
of the World Economic Forum Global Shapers
Community. He regularly facilitates workshops
on business design, entrepreneurship and social
innovation.

FERNANDO G. ALBERTI

Fernando G. Alberti is President of **strategique**.
Institutes Council Leader at Professor Michael E.
Porter's Microeconomics of Competitiveness affiliate
faculty network, Harvard Business School, he is a
tenured full professor of Strategic Entrepreneurship
at LIUC (Italy), where he chairs the Institute for
Entrepreneurship and Competitiveness.

Former Industrial Strategist for the World Bank and
UNIDO, he regularly advises firms and institutions on
strategy, entrepreneurship and competitiveness issues.

STRATEGIQUE

strategique is an international think thank, based at Harvard, focusing on entrepreneurial, innovative and strategic process that accelerate competitiveness.

We are an international team of academics, entrepreneurs, consultants and policy makers who use a creative and innovative mindset combined with a business design approach to the analysis, execution and development of innovative business models; and the study, research and publication of the most actual strategic and entrepreneurial contents, tools, methodologies, and applied knowledge to accelerate competitiveness.

We collaborate closely with different research institutes and think tanks worldwide, primarily with the Institute for Strategy and Competitiveness directed by Prof. Michael E. Porter, at Harvard Business School, where we are based.

strategique designs your future, today.

CONTACT US:

info@strategique.us
www.strategique.us
Harvard Square. 1 Mifflin Pl. Suite 400
Cambridge, MA 02138

Printed in France by Amazon
Brétigny-sur-Orge, FR

19114095R00067